Uncertain Shores

Poetry by
John Marks

First published by Busybird Publishing 2023

Copyright © 2023 John K Marks

ISBN: 978-1-922954-61-9

This book is copyright. Apart from any fair dealing for the purposes of study, research, criticism, review, or as otherwise permitted under the Copyright Act, no part may be reproduced by any process without written permission. Enquiries should be made through the publisher.

This is a work of fiction. Any similarities between places and characters are a coincidence.

Cover image: Christine Marks

Cover design: Busybird Publishing

Layout and typesetting: Busybird Publishing

Editor: Krystle Herdy

Busybird Publishing
2/118 Para Road
Montmorency, Victoria
Australia 3094
www.busybird.com.au

Dedication

This book of memory and verse for
Benjamin and Bianca is dedicated to
Christine (1945-2007),
whose last Christmas card's image and words
were the inspiration for *Uncertain Shores*.

*'Wishing that all your
personal storms will
pass quickly so that
each & every Christmas
& new year will be
happier & more content.'*

…For we are but travellers
on uncertain shores.

Special thanks to Ngee Chee for her
kindness and understanding and to
Dr. Tarni Jennings for her invaluable guidance
all those years ago.

Contents

Uncertain Shores
Uncertain Shores	2
An Unsinkable Boat	4
A Day of Passing Storms	5
Lessee and Lessor	6
Beach (Sand in the Clam)	7
On the Road	8
Going Down	9

Ark of Fools
Egypt	14
Delphi	15
Patmos	16
Israel	17

Weekends of Sundays
Easter	20
Church Music	21
Sunday Lunch	22
Palm Sunday	23
The Sunday Roast	24
Liebesträume	26
The Dog and the Lean Man	27
Answers Scientific	28
The Apple Orchard	29
Adoration	30
Under the Smug Moon	31
When Marx Met Engels	32
The Rope	33

Life on the Edge
Ambush (Vietnam, 1969)	36
As You Pass By	37
Every Step	38
The Dust of His Vietnam	39

A Postcard	40
Recovery	41
The Bus Stop	42
War	43
No Music	44

Coming Home to the Dance

Coming Home to the Dance	46
All He Asked	47
Tears in Her Eyes	48
The Drill	49
They Prayed for a Miracle	50
Memorial	52
The Rabbit Shoot	53
Here or There	54
On April Day	55
Wounded	56
Fragments	58
Non Compos Mentis	59
Sleep Was a Memory	60
Not Now	61

Things We Share

Things We Share	64
Obsession	65
Vladivostok	66
Love in the Country	67
Winter	68
Spring	69
Take Care	70
The Earth Moved	71
Last Day (April 19th 2007)	72
April 20th 2007	73
Visitations	74
Dark No More	75
Birthday Flowers	76
Christine	77
Empty Chairs	78
Adrift	79

Retired	80
Home Sweet Home	81
Nature Ever-Changing	82
Heaven or Hell	83
To Dream	84

UNCERTAIN SHORES

UNCERTAIN SHORES

When we come to the end of work and play
and watch the orange fire on the night sea fade,
we drift with ease in the cool of a soft sea breeze.
While pendulums clock our measured hours,
we summon the seashore days of songs and flowers,
'When all the birds of the air fell a sighing and a—'

Those old songs, worn out with singing.
Old vases of dead flower stems
on gravestones in fields of thistles and burrs
in sand dune scrub where the sun is warm.
Nature in harmony with the velvet murmur of oceans,
content with the wreckage of sailing ships.

The hot, dry summers. The milk bar. The convent bells.
Mornings of green-mirrored sea sunlit with white fire.
On the shell-grit beach, brittle with kelp, seaweed and lice
where, standing with fog at her feet, she rang the handbell
to call the nuns in from their morning swim in the shallows,
where, at lap's edge, seagulls floated on feathered air
while children played elsewhere, on seesaws and swings.

They spoke of the white horses of the sea,
the drumming thunder and reckless charge of breakers,
of the great waves of foam and sea spray. Squadrons of
cavalry rushing headlong to the sandstone barricades
to withdraw, suck back, gather, and come again,
their banners flying, the white horses of the sea.

The burning sun and dry wind storms of sharp silica sand.
Coasts of sea-wrack tangles of fish bones and dead gulls.
Barnacle tents on twisted pylons in seagrass walls.
Boulevards of umbrellas, scaffolds of ribs and rags.
Promenades of houses and churches in sandhill scrub.
Doorbells in hallways, all cobwebs and rust.

They had walked the cliffs of sandstone cracks and limestone stacks
in best trousers and flapping coats. And with hats in hand, they
stood hard against the rising wind, towers of sea, spray and foam,
where, on the dark and miserable brine, masted ships heaved.
Beyond the windows of buried churches, sea winds sweep
sand, scrub, thistles and burrs over graveyards of stones.
On these uncertain shores, travellers rest alone.

AN UNSINKABLE BOAT
The Agony of errors

The orchestras played music to the spheres;
tenor, soprano, basso profundo each gave it their all,
thrilling those who could hear. Curtain calls and
flowers for all as the earth sank below the sea.

The devout heard that the *meek shall inherit the earth*.
They cooked the books, made profits untold,
built their temples of awe,
pitied and prayed for the weak and the poor, but still
asked for more as the earth sank below the sea.

The wealthy few— kept alive beyond their years—
declared, 'Some of us will be left, and it best be me!'
'What good's the insurance and havens tax-free?'
As the earth sank below the sea.

The Earth, like the Titanic, was thought an unsinkable ship where
life was all party and pose. In quickstep-time, the music flowed
until an iceberg surprise stole the show and holed the boat.
The band played at a fearful pace, hymns of hope upon the slope
until they gurgled and choked, and all went down with the
unsinkable boat.

A DAY OF PASSING STORMS

It was too far, and the journey ended.
We had travelled the Coorong Road
together in better days,
but all I felt was the sea breeze chill
from the window open to the
incoming storm on the bay.

Those days at the Caledonian;
the beer and tobacco, the push
and swirl of rough men and poets,
women in their fine floras.
Days of loud discourse. Of laughter.
Of promises made. Of dreams.

To the cries of lovers caught in a rush
of blustering wind and stinging sand,
with the roar of night waves, surging, pounding,
and the scraping wash of retreating sea,
I found my way against the chill of rain
to a house on the sand shores of Rivoli Bay.

In the darkness, beyond the headland,
flying sooted clouds joined the sea,
scudding the yellow moon to lurid green.
Ocean waves thundered ashore,
howling winds and roaring seas colliding in
twisted nets of hail and driving rain,
hammering hard and fast,
curtaining the salted window glass.

LESSEE AND LESSOR

They came with armchairs and were given land to keep,
and with savage intent, forests went cheap
to parklands for sheep and parrots of mostly red and green.
Foxglove flowers in gardens of forget-me-not blue,
cool summer showers upon lilac hills and pastures of a
dull green hue.
A plague of locusts on the wing mistook the summer for spring,
chewed the wheat and stripped bare every beautiful thing.

Ravens and crows in widow's weeds gathered in rows
on escarpments of sunlit gold where eagles stayed out of reach
but were shot at close range, feeding on fly-blown sheep.
With rifles ready and stirrup irons gleaming, the Colonial Rats
cut loose in the chase to bring down their prey—
mostly emus, they'd say.

The landlord, the lessor, kept the books and counted the cost
of flour and tea and of blankets, with smallpox and measles
given free to the indigenous lessees,
who were not counted but died unseen.
Those Colonial Rats who lived off the sheep's back,
who murdered with ease, grew ravenous weeds and let vermin
run free,
now decompose in tranquil repose beneath monuments of
polished stone.

But the Indigenous people, custodians of this ancient and
fragile land,
cut the chains of colonial servitude, poverty and disease,
and, with a gathering voice, said NO to privilege and wealth.
NO to those in parliaments, who decompose in tranquil repose,
still thinking they can do as they please
in the year of two-thousand and twenty-three.

BEACH (SAND IN THE CLAM)

I used to like the beach:
the sand, the sun, the breeze.
I'd paddle like a drowning dog
in the shallows of a roaring sea.
I used to take her and more.
We'd lie in the glare of sun,
she in a two-piece and I in a one.
Sand and flesh together.

All that changed
when body shape altered.
Sand flies grew larger,
jellyfish and sharks cruised by,
sand swirled and gouged the crotch,
stuck to everything.
Ultraviolets soared to cancer level,
so we left the beach.

Now we see beached crowds on TV.
Umbrellas, shelters, bats and balls.
Bathers lying near-naked, no tops at all,
soaking up the sun, smothered in UV block.
Bronzed Anzacs parade in flimsy shorts,
privates near exposed,
all the while the polluted sea
draws the swimmers in.

I still visit every year or so—
in decent shorts and a hat to match—
to paddle in happy disrepair.
Back then, ultraviolets did not matter,
and sharks were yet to turn Jurassic.
Now, dog turds dry where they drop,
so I flee the beach of rotting kelp and slimy rock
in miserable disrepair.

ON THE ROAD

With banners triumphant, the tyrants came
with murder in mind and with deep regret.
They built walls of concrete and barbwire
to alleviate our poverty and sharpen our minds.
We served the state, the alchemists of crime,
changing base metal to gold and water to wine.
Going nowhere on the road to somewhere.

Walls, windows, and blinds;
park benches, blankets, and stars;
deserts, tents, no water to spare,
decimated forests and rivers of mud.
Slum cities, shanties for all,
these, our refuges after the fall.
Going nowhere on the road to somewhere.

Heavy our burden on roads untrodden.
In forests of dark rain, we saw rainbows.
In deserts, we saw constellations of stars.
In nature's cathedrals of dancing fire,
we stood and cried out with one voice,
'Who will relieve us of our suffering?'
Going nowhere on the road to somewhere.

On bitter, lonely roads, we travel
with our souls stripped bare.
Will we ever breathe abundant air,
or will we hear an echo of our voices
on a road somewhere, going nowhere?

GOING DOWN

Measured tides
beat time
suck back out of time
sea shells
jingle shells
angel wings
Aristotle's lanterns
on sea shores
of chopsticks
and take-away things
A clatter of matter
Going down

Tinkling piano
notes run
on waters clear
for fish to shine
in the slime
of their muddy shrines
catching
fragile notes
strung
on withering vines
Going down

Skies rumble
waterfalls
in buckets
tumble
rattle and roar
on granite walls
Cascades of rainbows
brighten the sun
caught in snares
sweeping

xylophone stairs
Going down

Drones of brass bees
bumble on the hum
dragonflies float
on gossamer wings
disturbing
metallic ducks
on rippling ponds
with other ducks
Pacific blacks
and common browns
Going down

In rafts of dry leaves
high in tall trees
squawking fledglings
demand feeding
but are beaten and eaten
by scooping swooping
beak smacking snacking
brown pelicans
Going down

In whirlwinds
of feathers
pigeons go
to drop a glop
on buildings
and pose
while cities die
in the destruction
of construction
Glockenspielists
build towers of glass
for high-paying

satisfied baboons
who still think
storks deliver
babies at noon
Balloons
Going down

Skies rumble
tumble upside down
Oceans of yellow seas
gurgle and thrash
with mashings
of plasticine sludge
Fishermen's nets
trap dolphins, turtles
and angry whales
Great catches of fish
chemically bound
sold as sound
to rich and poor
and as fish dinners
for their cats
Those good old days
No more feasting
on lobster and crab
now it's just chips
all 'round
The myth of plenty
Going down

ARK OF FOOLS

EGYPT

With waving crowds, some in prayer and loud song,
brave Noah launched his ark upon the sea,
a ship of fools for the wasted lands to see.

But it all went wrong with champagne brawls and flying thongs;
the devout blamed the choir for inappropriate jests,
and the captain lost his bearings and set a course due west.

The crew with charts askew headed east to the nearest shore,
where they saw the poor and oppressed in desert camps onshore
and waved a cheery goodbye while feasting on lobster and cod.

On to Cairo, a mystery of dynasties, statues and rock-solid gods;
of kings and pharaohs of staring stone,
colonnades and temples with hieroglyphs sown.

The great pyramids:
stacks of chiselled stone to make a point
for Pharaohs Khufu, Khafre and Menkaure.

Flies, dust and hot desert sands ruined their style,
so they left the ancient pile, Cairo and the delta of the Nile
for the philosophical climes of Greece.

DELPHI

Upon a high and lofty mountain,
Walter cleared his throat
and gurgled his spit.
He tuned his chords to get the pitch,
and with feet firm on Delphi's ancient stones,
sang two slow notes and choked.

Smitten with Sophoclean verse, Walt changed his tone.
Going down on one knee with purpose, he moaned
to address the thousands on the windswept tiers of stone.
In eloquent tone and narcissistic woe, every word he played,
but his voice was weak, and he knew not where it strayed.

Distraught and dismayed, Echo heard naught of this soliloquy,
so the Oracle of Delphi spoke in a clear, loud tone,
'You're no Oedipus Rex! Get up, you fool!'
Walt swung about in awful fright,
and there she was, that diaphanous sprite,
and they left for Patmos that very same night.

PATMOS

Patmos, that desolate rock
where Saint John, in better days,
wrote of visions, revelations of doom and angelic festoons.
In his ghoulish shelter, a cave of dark and dank rock,
mould had rotted the recent ancient cloths.

In the hush of low light, they poked about, and
the choir gestured at the monastery and wandered out.
From the cave of dark rock came curses obscene
and loud shouts from the devout who remained unseen.

Some curious heads took a hard knock
upon Saint John's low-slung holy rock,
so on a steep and deep decline, they left Patmos
with bruised heads and worried minds.

No beast with horns or trumpet calls,
just a few wild goats and a strong sea squall.

ISRAEL

To the Holy Lands they came,
perplexed to see artefacts broken and cracked,
stone tablets of wise cuneiform polished black.
A thousand years of war and grinding dust
had obliterated any philosophical crust.
They read with intent translations of texts BC,
ancient words from King James' holy book, 1603 AD.

The hands-in-pockets choir strolled along the tragic way.
Bethlehem was under siege; no shepherds nor sheep to stray.
Barbed wire fences and locked holy sites,
rockets and starbursts and curfewed nights.

On board the ark, in a sparkle of light, they tangoed unsure
and forgot the oppressed in the slums onshore.
Blessed by a fresh sea breeze, they prepared to go.
The irascible choir sang sea chanties with gusto
while the devout held tight to relics between their knees
as the ark sailed from sight on turbulent seas.

WEEKENDS OF SUNDAYS

EASTER

Sunday morning pandemonium,
with crow craw and currawong song,
warbling magpies and black bird sing-alongs,
with a clanging peel of bells from
Calvin's lofty spires and Catholic peels.
Below the low churched hills, the town wakes
to fire sirens, howling dogs and bushfire smoke.

Pyjamaed and coffee-drenched in the lizard-warming sun
in my garden of rotting apples and fading blooms,
in a flurry of autumn leaves of amber-gold,
a magpie acapella, in priestly pose, beaks the air,
trilling discordant harmonies at the tolling of Easter bells
like sweet bells jangled, out of tune and harsh.[1]

---

1 From William Shakespeare's *Hamlet*

CHURCH MUSIC

The choir sang
the organ roared
and they sang some more
until every hallowed stone
and entablature was caressed
with choirs of Heldentenors
in Babylonian splendour

SUNDAY LUNCH

He chucked it on
with blackened hairy arm:
cheese, tomatoes and
a slice of tinned spam.
Added a lump or two
of tropical fruit
(pineapple, at a guess),
extra cheese
to cover the mess and
garlic with chilli to bless.
Cooked to a crisp,
it arrived hot and flat,
but that's mostly
how Sundays are.

PALM SUNDAY

Lovely Sunday Jane
led the boys in respectful prayer,
but their prayers were of
manic crowds waving palms
and Tarzan saving Jane
from rampaging rhinos.
On the edge of doom,
the lesson ended.

With a hullabaloo, like
overstimulated chimps,
the Sunday boys helter-skeltered
through calcimined halls Presbyterian.
Grey suits, white shirts, tartan ties
(Clan unknown),
socks loose in black boots,
they ran to the rose gardens of perfumes.

Branches broken, thorns snapped off,
the biggest spat on, stuck to the nose.
Dust swirling, hair flying, clothes holed,
rhinos charged each other with rose horns,
chased by Sunday matrons,
a bald man with a garden hose
and widowed rose growers
to as far as their front gates.

Then, in whooping clouds of late summer dust,
the Sunday boys disappeared, as they must,
into a street of gardens old with neglect,
of war palms, wild rosemary and weeds,
where, from windows tall, old men and widows spied
on the memories of youth passing by,
alive to the hymn *Abide with Me*
from the Sunday brass at practice on the oval:
trombone, euphonium, cornet and tuba.

THE SUNDAY ROAST

By the crackling fire, the bright sparks flew.
Cypress logs do that, but not so the dinner crew.
They settled to yarn about war and troubled times and
savoured the taste of the pan drippings, and then,
for whatever reason, Rudyard Kipling came to light.
They all knew a couple of lines,
so with rowdy enthusiasm, each outdoing the other, recited,
'Then it's Tommy this, an' Tommy that, an' 'Tommy, 'ow's yer soul?'
'But it's "Thin red line of 'eroes" when the drums begin to roll…'

Then, it was on to Wellington's victory and Napoleon's defeat.
'Such slaughter and butchery; twenty thousand horses dead.'
'Anyone for Beef Wellingtons?' A silent shaking of heads at
such a tasteless remark that fell flat and lapsed into
ordinary thought.
With their intellects astray, they speculated on but confused
the American Civil War with the American Revolution.
They agreed the British red coats were useless—
as was mad King George—
and then they sang without conviction, *'John Brown's body lies
a-mouldering in the grave'* and *'Whose idea was it anyway?'*

With nothing more to add, they poked at the fire and
drifted in the warmth and comfort of their digested roast
while stamping out sparks on the mat beneath their feet.
From an armchair out of reach, a voice of concern croaked,
recalling the wreckage of ships caught in South Sea squalls.
'The lost souls,' he opined. *'And we shouldn't forget the others ashore:
George, James, Arthur, and brother Jack.'* But the list fell short.
They held their suspicions and darkest thoughts
lest they harm the fragile memories of family lore.

Somewhere in the house of hewn stone and wood planks,
a clock chimed the late hour in two distinct tones.
In no hurry to go, they arose at a leisurely pace,
only to be taken in by a menagerie of sixty-three birds
of splendid plumage perched in a cabinet of glass and wood.
They had seen it all before but liked to comment on the way out.
'Taxidermy is such a skill.' 'How did he capture and kill?'
'One hundred and twenty-six glass eyes of every shape and size,'
And whatever they could think of next.

With a fair bit of phlegm, someone suggested it was time to go.
They thanked the wife for the delicious bread pudding
but forgot to mention the roast.
Collecting their hats and coats at the back door,
they delayed some more for a bit of a chat.
It was suggested that tomorrow being Monday,
perhaps they would like to stay to help with washing day.
With a push and a shove, they left in a gaggle and a cheery,
'Not likely are we offering to do that!'

LIEBESTRÄUME

In the blue delphinium light,
a dry summer's garden in rapture sings
with insects on the wing.
Rainbow lorikeets, plumaged bright,
squabble and screech in the afternoon light.

Hairnets and shawls and stockings that fall
in shoes down at heel, the not-so-tall
choir 'round the piano sings with harmonic bliss
until the soprano clenches her fist and
strikes a half dozen high notes that missed.

Lorikeets, like arrows, fly in rainbow twists,
caterpillars shrivel and drop, and
iridescent lizards slip from their rocks.
Spiders without cobwebs play knock-knock.

The choir retires to try the pastrami while
the pianist regains her composure
to play with indelicate flare the *Liebestrami*.

Like Liszt's piano notturno,
the ennui of summer fades
into crepuscular light
and mosquito nights.

THE DOG AND THE LEAN MAN

The lean grey man
eyebrows the path,
leading his old brown dog.
Then, the happy dog leads
to snuff the grass,
cocks without result and
looks up and about.

The lean man sniffs the air,
not the dog.

At the intersection, they stand,
all six legs in a shared tangle.
Off again, one leading the other
through the smoke haze of evening fires.
The lean man and the old dog
come and go, one leading the other
through the shadows of winter trees.

ANSWERS SCIENTIFIC

I didn't fail my exam.
Only my answers were different:
unexpected and mysterious.
The examiners were perplexed.

I should have said,
On a glorious spring day,
the lilac was in full mauve
with a chorus of singing bees.

In the sweetness of that honeyed air,
I drifted into the sacred centre of my soul
while a gentle breeze feathered the pages
for answers scientific.

THE APPLE ORCHARD

A fruitless orchard
bent and twisted
left to run
bared of leaf
budding poorly
no fruit to come

Bright flocks
descend to beak
clean the dying buds
flash and fly
to hasten
the death of another

ADORATION

Elaeocarpus adored Pandorea,
blue berry fruits he offered;

in turn, she entwined his reaching arms
in profusions of pink, delicate blooms.

In the summer of their becoming,
they were admired at Valentine's.

Beautiful together in married bliss,
Pandorea shone in garlands bright.

But when Elaeocarpus branched out, ready to flee,
Pandorea's twining beauty began to wilt.

With wanton embrace, Pandorea
smothered and tightly bound Elaeocarpus.

Expectations were duly met
with her vibrant flowering days,

but being so tightly bound
with overwhelming adoration,
married bliss died with strangulation.

UNDER THE SMUG MOON
For Ngee

My lady of curves,
a mystery in black.

Her seductive beauty exposed
in a smear of soft rain.

Under the smug moon,
hesitating to speak,

she slips into the night
of shadows and mist.

Caught at the corner light,
she hesitates, then vanishes from sight.

WHEN MARX MET ENGELS
For Baxter

When Karl met Friedrich of late,
he was not in a congenial state;
his socialist leanings had taken a beating
in a bottle of bourgeois red,
but Karl spotted his chance
and offered a socialist red instead.

With a flurry of salted wisecracks
and deepest of darkest thoughts,
they lost the plot in a palaver of stratagems.
Das Kapital was to be the panacea,
but they remembered not a jot.

Their exploration of socialist leanings
needed a fair bit of kneading,
so they poured a Bolshevik red with meaning
and declared with fisted tumblers raised
that the bourgeoisie were wallowing in ideological pap,
while the lumbering proletariat danced the bourree to all that.

THE ROPE

Sweat
washed clean,
he was
horribly bent
with
murderous intent.
With a soap on a rope,
past eight,
or
was it past nine?
Whatever it was,
he was late
for his date
with a soap on a rope
in a knot
in his crotch.

LIFE ON THE EDGE

AMBUSH (VIETNAM, 1969)

Crickets, one by one, sing
in the dark canopies of jungle trees,
then, all together, scream like fire sirens.
Birds carol to join the din. Last light falls,
monkeys howl, and the pandemonium ends
in the pitch-black of wandering night
where snakes taste the air and wait,
and scorpions are somewhere.

A hot breeze, acrid with charcoal smoke,
alerts the sleepers in the canopies, rattles an army
of brittle swamp reeds, then dies in a shuffle.
The sloe-black night holds and threatens
while the late, cold moon shines clear and silver
on a tangled wash of fog, blue silhouettes of trees,
bamboo jungles and far-off indigo hills.

In the clouded hours before dawn, all is still
until, on the low horizon, first light cuts razor-sharp
through swirls of rising mist. The blue shadows lift,
and the jungle grows from mauve to ashen green.
In the breathless chill of morning air, riflemen wait.

The pale moon fades into the lilac sky
as the monumental dome of the red sun rises
to a murderous applause of machine gun and rifle fire.
Three men lay dead. One was cornered and shot.
His brain, wet with red stain, lays in his shattered skull,
the shard of missing part some yards away.

Another day has begun in the dust
and the heat and the sweat
of South Vietnam.

AS YOU PASS BY

You tread the paths of war
by reading history books of debatable facts,
of battle honours and killings,
pictures of carnage and nature tossed
on battlefields of dust and ash
where children starve, and mothers weep,
and where, in victory, soldiers die and lay in heaps.

From afar, you inhale the polluted air of war,
knowing we are not or cannot go that way.
Look to where the headstones lay.
Walk the paths and avenues of stones and,
as you pass by the battlefields and memorials with
uneasy steps, say their names, hear their voices,
and listen to the echo, the echo of wasted bones.

EVERY STEP

I made her a promise and said goodbye
in the darkness that hour before dawn.

In the mess hut, at first light, we gathered
for breakfast to reflect on the spectre of death,

no lights or cigarettes to indicate our going.
With the bitter brew downed, it was time to go.

In the half-light, we filed out beyond the wire
in a cloud of damp summer dust.

Every step was an endless goodbye.

THE DUST OF HIS VIETNAM

Through the dust of his Vietnam,
he was dragged and dropped
in the yellow clay sand.
He lay soaked in death's fine sweat
and final dust, a wounded VC man.

We stood close about
while his wound was bound.
In a turn-away glance,
I caught his stare of hate,
or was it his despair or mine?
His entire life had come
and, in that moment of recognition,
life and death belonged.

Through choking dust and diesel fumes,
armoured carriers came.
He was gathered from the dust
and carried to the ramp and gaping door.
With a shuffle of combat boots on dead leaves
and a low chorus of *a one, a two and a three*,
they let the wounded man go.
He flew and broke on a wall of steel.

I saw a dying pale man splayed,
slide and drop before the door closed.
In spinning clouds of yellow dust, he went.
And, when the blatteration died,
there was only the sunlit dust
beneath the rubber trees of his Vietnam.

A POSTCARD

At evening close,
in their shut-down house,
work and school days ended,
the wood stove sparked and the kettle boiled,
thoughts drifted no further than the kitchen table
with its pickings of mutton, potatoes, onions and cheese.
Conversations stared ahead until his voice cut through,
'Ah, well —another day — we will get there — someday."

But luck and sunnier days were not for them.
The empire had called. The farms were left to grow weeds.
The farm dogs barked, each in turn and to each other.
Brass band music and bagpipe swirl kept them steady,
while on the battlefields, men lay wounded in the mud
and stench, where they bled until they were dead.
In their shut-down house, they grew old with their dreams,
played their music, passed away and were forgotten.

All that remained was a postcard with a line or two:
We are doing well in this empty and hostile land.
Miss you all back home. Grandpa passed away April last.
Everyone's as well as can be expected.
Love from everyone here,
Happy Christmas
Emily

A kangaroo stamp and Union Jack on a postcard never sent.

RECOVERY

Thighs like smooth rolling hills.
Valleys and gullies of bristles and pox.
Knuckles like rocks, knotted and cramped.
Blue roses bloom in circles of dark blood.
Vultures in white spats squabble about facts.
Eagles in elegant flight wear black tights.
In constellations of stars and black holes,
there is music that is hard to beat.
I recommend the Helicopter Quartet as a treat.

Recovery should reside in these strange lines,
but if it is too much and you are in decline,
fear not, for there must be better lines than mine.
So, under the grey blankets of swollen night,
my pillowed head is at peace
with a grimace of smiling teeth.

THE BUS STOP

Six men in great coats and slouch hats
slow-march, the coffin on shoulders high.
Sliding black boots on bitumen gliding.
No sound of marching on the rain-swept road.
Layer upon layer, through fields of dark rain,
to the bus stop they came.

With precise and practised drill,
the coffin passes shoulder to shoulder.
Six men in great coats and slouch hats
slow march, the coffin on shoulders high,
through layer upon layer of pitiless rain,
storm clouds blacker than the bitumen track.

Under a canopy of black umbrellas,
mourners, blacker still, crowd the edge.
In the parting light, the rites are read.
A rifle volley sounds amidst squalls of rain and hail,
and mourners in black coats, their umbrellas askew,
rush through windswept curtains of curving dark rain.

On a black and stormy afternoon
at the bus stop, six men keep watch,
and, at the passing of the deluge,
infantrymen in great coats and slouch hats
return to the barracks across fields
of sodden grass sludge and sliding mud.

WAR

Life
on the edge

Life
on a sharp edge

Life
without an edge

NO MUSIC

I march with blind eyes
through cheering crowds of darkness.
No hymns, no music,
only the whispering chatter,
a chorus of the dead and the dying.

COMING HOME TO THE DANCE

COMING HOME TO THE DANCE

When the fighting ended, he turned up home,
shaped and bent by the war.
He joined the dance to tango with them,
but the military two-step was his ken.
He tried once more, whirling
in quick step time with a dance all of his own.
So, they left him stranded on the dance floor,
spinning in the gore of his private war.
With dance steps too many, he stumbled
and went back to where he had been before:

Everywhere was dusted cream with dry summer clay.
Damp tarpaulin tents, sandbag walls and canvas beds.
Morning fog low on bamboo jungles of thorns.
Yellow butterflies on pink blooms in rusted barbed wire.
Days of dung and dust and the sweet, pungent stench of corpses.
A violent crack, a yellow flash, and he was crushed to a slither.

Damaged and bitter, he tells all
to those who pause to hear
how he fought against the odds
and how he had danced for them.
Now, in the cold nights on the streets,
he dances alone on crippled bones,
wearing his medals with pride,
asking simply to be known.

ALL HE ASKED

In the national interest,
to the war zone he was sent,
counting not on dying soon.
But he met death full on.
In panic and fright and
with his brains rearranged,
he came back at midnight
to make his way home.
He wandered the old roads
and arrived at a gate familiar.
With a handshake, they said,
'You're back,' and that was that.
An arm around the shoulder
was all he asked,
to steady him, to hold him back
from the edge of doom,
but he had counted not
on love dying so soon.

TEARS IN HER EYES

I loved a stranger,
though she never was.
I played my part in war,
saw violent death first-hand,
explained with fervour my desires,
but I failed to see the tears in her eyes
and closed the door to mine.

THE DRILL

A shot.
I practise the drill
and hit the ground hard, feeling ill.
Face down in the dirt to avoid the shots,
but in my backyard, a war zone there is not.
So, quickly, I stand with foolish stare,
and the children ask, 'What are you doing there?'
They willingly tell the happy fact,
'It was just a whip crack to scare the cats!'
I reply, 'I cannot stand cats,
so can we leave it at that?'

THEY PRAYED FOR A MIRACLE

In the lounge near the front door,
they sat like stone amongst bric-a-brac
and a palm in a jardinière on the floor
until a voice from the cabinet radio came.
They strained to hear and forward-bent
to catch the midday news.
The war was in their favour but not going well.
The weather was dry, with dark blue skies
and gathering clouds as well.

The men left by the front door
while the women stayed to talk some more,
to consider the war and where he might be.
His photo, a black and white passe-partout,
by the party line phone on the wall
where romantic Egypt also hung.
Tall of frame, all pyramids and palms,
camels and wise men lost
in a desert of yellow ochre sand.

In the party line queue, three rings were their call,
but the clatter of bells were few.
They hung on 'til the end of the war
and prepared a welcome home for him
at the front door.
They waited for the very last train,
but a letter came in the mailbag drop
with official words of grief:
survived the Middle East. Burma claimed him.
Lost without trace, Singapore named him missing.

They prayed for a miracle
and kept an eye on the front door.
Romantic Egypt rotted in the frame
and was consigned to the flames.
The party line phone was torn off the wall
and sent to the shed out the back.
They had to accept he would never be found.
The farm was sold, and on the way out,
they lifted him down from the nail in the wall.

MEMORIAL

At embarkation parade, their only son
heard an officer say, 'Good luck. Some of you
may not be coming home, but be assured,
your name will be forever known, etched in memorial stone.'

Somewhere among the chiselled dead
is his name, which starts not with A or Z.
His war had lasted but a lonely hour,
where, in a flash of terror, he was blown to bits.

At Christmas, to a charge of raised glasses, they turn
to the photo of their only child, lost and far from home.
At Easter, they looked to the cross and the flame
to thank God for a life chiselled in memorial stone.

THE RABBIT SHOOT

Young men with slug guns
pumped pellets into rattling chains
of running tin rabbits and hares
with their rifles aimed true
to prove they still had the eye
from all those years at war.
Not tin rabbits and hares back then,
but running men, cut down in battle.
'It was either them or us,' they said.

They had shot rabbits before,
but in war, there was blood and gore,
the like never seen before.
So, with ferocious eyes, they aimed
to get their prize at the fair.
If they missed, they paid for more lead and
shot fast and loose until the money ran out;
no prizes for them.

A marksman who never served
shot every tin rabbit and hare
with nonchalant flair.
The boys laid down their guns in despair
and walked the trenches at the sideshow fair.
They had won the war but lost the game.
Their nightmares and fame were as
bittersweet as the toffee apples
freely given to the men who were there.

HERE OR THERE

In their youth, they took all before them,
but here they were, weathered and war-weary,
grey-suited and black-booted with medals pinned.
A battalion of ten leads a thousand dead men.
In time and line, they parade with rhythm and rhyme
past church walls, dark halls, and *cuppa-tea* stalls.

These are the haunted men with faraway eyes,
lost in a morass of adventures they cannot share,
still carrying the regiment's banner of battles fair
on the road to a Jerusalem that was neither here nor there.
It was all just a lie to give them the courage to die,
either here with neglect or over there under treacherous fire.

ON APRIL DAY

She hears the clarion call
and knows she will never know.
Dressed in soft lavender
and the pink flowers of her dreams,
she waits at the pick-up zone on April day.

He hears the clarion call
and knows she will never know.
He waits in his wheelchair
under a veranda with his hat on
at the pick-up zone on April day.

On April day, in the
cold light of dawn,
shoulder to shoulder,
arm in arm, they hold on
to the memories they know,
and he hears the clarion call
from the battlefields of long ago
when bravery and murder were all the go.

WOUNDED

In the hallways
of our lives,
grandfathers
kept time
until their springs broke,
and we drifted
into the misfortunes of war.

Beyond the windows,
we heard the voices
of the wounded,
'God with us. God with us.'
Grey, untidy men
shuffled to the end,
but before the bend,
they walked the black slate
of habit and stain
in churches of state,
and in rose gardens,
they wept in the rain.

When the killings were enough,
we built memorials with
crosses slung high
to celebrate the lost
but not the
living corpses of men
and wandering dead.

We took the applause,
missed our steps,
their smiles and loving arms.
We marched to the music
toward the end,
but before the bend,
asked God to be with us
but not with those
who did not go;
you who sent us
to our end.

FRAGMENTS

I went to war
with my banner flying
and came back
with the fragments
of my dreams

NON COMPOS MENTIS

In my madness, there was
darkness without end.

Thick and immovable
blankets of silent pestilence.

Vaporous apparitions
knocked at the sockets,

but there was nothing to see,
nothing to hang on to,

only shadows and delusions
and dreams never-ending.

Dear God, let me sleep.

SLEEP WAS A MEMORY

Sleep was a memory.
At four, I spat pale blood
and returned like an old shuffler
to a hotbed of left memories.
With sheets of sweat and sour vinegar,
I drifted through the long, lonely nights,
fighting wars on all fronts,
waking in the early hours
in floods of tears for moments
never held but wished for.

Too late to ask forgiveness
for the drink and absent days.
Her leaving frightened me.
Alone in fractured sleep,
in the kindness of the dark,
her soft voice came, but I failed to listen
and began grovelling and apologising,
just wanting her back, but she was gone.
I wiped my tears on the bedsheet
and blamed the cold weather
for my sore eyes.

NOT NOW

It
would be
over
by now
except
for the dog.

It
was
a long way
down
but
the dog
knew that.

THINGS WE SHARE

THINGS WE SHARE
by Christine Marks

we never met,
you and I, but
when we have time to spare, to stare,
we share the sky.

our eyes on the horizon
where sky and land merge, the verge,
draws us together,
dreaming.

clouds formed for storms
rouse reaction
and shift direction
from staring to caring.

walking on earth,
we both cast shadows,
deepening the growing bond
of fondness within.

eating, drinking, sleeping,
waking or thinking,
we are in harmony;
I am your echo.

sighing, moaning
and breathing,
our distant hearts beat
in near silence,

and when we leave,
small parts of us stay and stray,
caught by the wind.
is this how we meet?

OBSESSION

Between the half and the striking,
waiting for the early light,
chasing unresolved misadventures,
remnants of longing and regret.

But for one.

In the hot summer of our time,
we fell into amorous love
with robust blindness and joy.
She had *something* important to say,
but it was put aside for another day.

That summer day never came.

The song and the singing that held us
on the long drive that summer
will always be—always be— a sad obsession,

but there is still *something* I need to know
before the hour strikes.

VLADIVOSTOK
For Isobel

Streets without names
buildings with no shame
in shadows without corners
with no one to blame

Vladivostok in the frame

LOVE IN THE COUNTRY

The moon on the full
dredged the pale green
country in shimmering blue,
sculpturing, in breathless
wonder, the land of
sparse trees and rabbit holes
where, in the hush of rabbity-night,
she put out the moon.

WINTER

A frustration of rain
a lull in the storm
dreadful silence
before the wind
whips to a frenzy
reluctant rain.

SPRING

Thousands of tiny
flowering stars
sparkling white
jutting forth
from insipid
green hedges
in the twilight.

TAKE CARE

If you go down a rabbit hole
in search of a kind, soft bunny,
you may find a beautiful monster instead.

THE EARTH MOVED

Her living and dying hung in a dripline.
Softly, she spoke from the shadows of evening,
'Take these rings, keep them safe.'
Those summer days of blue sapphire engagement
and the ache of young love slipped away
as the earth moved and the sun passed into night
where times past and present were one,
and overtures to future faded in sleep.

LAST DAY (APRIL 19th 2007)

She opened her eyes,
tried to speak
but only the sound
of her breath.

Her last words lost
on the last day,
on the last breath
of her existence.

APRIL 20th 2007

In the earliest hours
    of all my mornings
There was death
    in the dark lands
The wetlands
    The parklands
The wet roads
    The bleak house
The stairway
    and the door
Two keys to unlock
    an empty house
A meaningless shell
    of clocked time
Crippled with grief
    I dropped to my knees
A stranger
    on the doorstep
Of a house
    I once knew
And when the rain
    in torrents came
On the darkest
    of all my days
In wrapped arms
    I held her and wept

VISITATIONS

In the early hours, she came,
not of this world but
desirable still.
Once more, we slept,
her body pressing
with warmth and reassurance.
In the comfort and pleasure
of that ethereal moment,
I drifted into fathomless sleep,
waking in the quiet calm
of late morning.

DARK NO MORE

Now, in the dark,
I sleep awake
with my eyes open
to know the dark.

Through the dense black,
she came once more,
and with her last touch,
she closed both her eyes and mine,
and it was dark no more.

BIRTHDAY FLOWERS

The perfume of the mint bushes,
the soft blue of Algerian irises
and the pure whites at winter's end.

The wattles are coming on, but
she will miss their display
of gaudy yellow on her birthday.

CHRISTINE

It is often said
that loose ends be bundled,
completed and put away
to gather dust and move on.

But we gathered and met
because love has no end.
We placed her ashes
to loosen the ends.

Like ribbons in a soft breeze,
our memories of her
flow free to breathe, untangled.

EMPTY CHAIRS

happy new year.

at forty-one degrees
in a mausoleum
set with empty chairs
with no expectations,
for my love is but ashes,
cremated memories
in a box
on the sideboard.

Her watch
still keeps time.

happy new year.

such misery.

ADRIFT

A sibilation of monotones sing
in the darkness of tinnitus air.
In the cataract shadows of night,
floors and walls sway and give way
to moon shadow and star shine drifting slowly
over the wasteland of dried-up memories
where only the music flows. The whole gamut,
staccato, forte, pianissimo, slow fade
in a confabulation of halcyon days
of myth and murmur, of wind and waves.
Now, in ages old, nights eternal
adrift in anodyne sleep.

RETIRED

He rolls the grit
from his eyes
to see dawn's
weak blue screen,
hears the songbirds'
faded screams and
watches as ravens,
black as endless night,
fly through winter's
gold-rusted clouds
of dust and ash.

HOME SWEET HOME

When there is nothing more,
no trappings to be paid for,
just the voice inside your head
and pools of light at the bedhead;
on papered walls of delicate stripes,
a dusty frame on nail and thread.
A tapestry of roses above your head
with *Home Sweet Home* in scripted thread.
A single light shade, a cobweb spider bed:

there is nothing more to be said.

NATURE EVER-CHANGING

Step away from the claustrophobia of
accumulated wrapped certainty
and the hum-drum of your dreams.

Embrace the certainty that,
in a world of uncertainty,
nature is ever-changing.

In this disconnected world of strangers,
love for others can be fleeting.
But no matter.

Wherever we meet as friends
or greet a stranger in the street,
there will always be the hope

that we will remember each other,
and with that spark of love,
our lives will be transformed.

HEAVEN OR HELL

There is no such thing
as heaven and hell.

It's only for me to tell:

the grating of the gate
or the tinkling of the bell?

TO DREAM

I had no stamina
to continue

but I could dream
words unknown

soar like an eagle
over landscapes of my making

The beautiful chaos
of memory

The exquisite agony
of loneliness

The untrammelled
vastness of thought

No horizons within reach

I have said it all
I am free

About the Author

Born in 1945 in Mount Gambier, South Australia.

John directed theatrical productions and performed in others with the Mt. Gambier Theatre Group throughout the 1960s to the 1980s.

He began his National Service in 1967, serving in the Vietnam War with the 5th Battalion (5RAR) in 1969, then returning to Australia the same year.

He was a newsreader and program presenter, part-time, on ABC regional radio and began writing poetry in the late 70s and early 80s, moving to Melbourne around the same time.

John was admitted to the Austin Repatriation Hospital in 2005 with severe depression and PTSD.

His beloved wife Christine died from cancer in 2007.

Recently, John compiled *Shadows and Light* in 2022 – an anthology of stories by eight veterans and their partners dealing with the trauma of PTSD.

Uncertain Shores (2023) is his first poetry collection and draws upon these experiences.

www.ingramcontent.com/pod-product-compliance
Lightning Source LLC
Chambersburg PA
CBHW041319110526
44591CB00021B/2841